He's Not Finished

ARLENE BROWN

InspiringVoices®

Copyright © 2016 Arlene Brown.

All rights reserved. No part of this book may be used or reproduced by any means, graphic, electronic, or mechanical, including photocopying, recording, taping or by any information storage retrieval system without the written permission of the author except in the case of brief quotations embodied in critical articles and reviews.

Inspiring Voices books may be ordered through booksellers or by contacting:

Inspiring Voices
1663 Liberty Drive
Bloomington, IN 47403
www.inspiringvoices.com
1 (866) 697-5313

Because of the dynamic nature of the Internet, any web addresses or links contained in this book may have changed since publication and may no longer be valid. The views expressed in this work are solely those of the author and do not necessarily reflect the views of the publisher, and the publisher hereby disclaims any responsibility for them.

Any people depicted in stock imagery provided by Thinkstock are models, and such images are being used for illustrative purposes only.
Certain stock imagery © Thinkstock.

ISBN: 978-1-4624-1190-0 (sc)
ISBN: 978-1-4624-1191-7 (e)

Library of Congress Control Number: 2016909164

Print information available on the last page.

Inspiring Voices rev. date: 7/19/2016

To my amazing family. You have been there
for me every step of the way.
Thank you.

In loving memory of Ray Rohrer, my brother in Christ

Contents

Introduction ix

Chapter 1: The Accident 1
Chapter 2: Early Years 15
Chapter 3: Circumstances 22
Chapter 4: Shepherd Center 24
Chapter 5: I'm Speaking! Are You Listening? 31
Chapter 6: He's Not Finished 35
Chapter 7: Home Sweet Home 40
Chapter 8: Where Do We Go from Here? 46

Introduction

No one expects to get up one day and experience a moment that will change one's life forever. One step, one decision, one moment in time—it happens in a split second. There is no turning back. When I woke up April 1, 2012, I did not expect, by any stretch of the imagination, it would be the day God would reshape who I was and where I was going. That is the kind of thing you read about in books, or is it?

This book is about an unexpected journey that has transformed my life. Join me as I take you through eighteen months of pain, heartache, and unbelievable joy that only faith in God could bring me through.

Chapter 1

The Accident

Was it Sunday already? Recently, every day seemed to move faster. I felt like I was trapped on a roller coaster. It was becoming more and more difficult to juggle family, work, and church responsibilities. Even a quick phone call to my best friend was almost nonexistent. Every week I seemed to get further behind with everything. I tried to take advantage of every minute I had. I woke up early every day so that I could start with a devotional time. Lately, there were more and more days when I wanted to hit the snooze button. But that was not going to help me get through another day. I really needed this time to focus on God.

I had a forty-five-minute commute to work, which I spent listening to K-LOVE, a Christian radio station, and to God, when He could get my attention. I had been praying that He would show me a way to make everything in my life work out. The stress was really getting to me. I had felt for several weeks that the Holy Spirit was encouraging me to ask for strength, wisdom, and courage. My thoughts would always go to the book of Joshua. Joshua is one of my favorite characters in the Bible. His faith and courage, exhibited while leading the Israelites into the Promised Land, had always been a great example to me. I didn't understand at the time why God was leading me like this, but later, as I thought back, it was very clear that God was preparing me for the rest of my life.

On Sunday, April 1, I woke up early. Darlene, my twin sister, and I went to early church and afterward I taught my women's Sunday school class. After church, I headed home to eat lunch and relax. Shawn, my stepson, was getting married that afternoon, but we were not going to the wedding. He and his fiancée had planned a small wedding with only their children, Ashley and Zach, attending.

When I arrived home, Bert, my husband, told me there was a change of plans. Shawn had called and wanted us to come to the wedding after all. That was perfect for me, because while I wanted to be at the wedding, I didn't want to impose. It was a beautiful spring day, perfect for a wedding.

We ate lunch and then drove to Shawn's house, where the wedding was to take place. Ashley, Zach, and their three children were there when we arrived. Since we were early, this gave us time to visit with our great-grandchildren before the wedding. Malachy and Julian were running around playing, so I picked up their four-month-old sister, Zaley.

The wedding was scheduled to begin at two o'clock. As the time approached, I went outside with Zaley to see what everyone was doing. When I walked outside, I noticed there were two decks. One deck was large and went straight off the back of the house. The other deck was narrow and wrapped around the side of the house. It was also much higher off the ground. Since this was my first visit to their house, I decided to walk around on the narrow deck to see if it went all the way around to the front of the house. As I stepped onto the deck, I felt my shoe catch on something. Before I realized what was happening, I began to fall forward against the railing. I could hear the wood crack as I fell against it. I tried to grab onto anything I could as I felt myself start to tumble forward.

My main concern now was Zaley. The odds of me surviving the fall were much better than hers. I wrapped my arms tightly around her as I fell to the ground. I heard someone scream. It may have been me. When we landed on the ground, my left arm fell open, and Zaley rolled away from me. She began to cry, and everyone came running. I wanted to get to her, but I couldn't move.

Have you ever been hit so hard you couldn't breathe or move? That's how I felt lying there on the ground. Details of those first few minutes were vague. I remember Ashley kneeling beside me. Bert was there too. Ashley told someone to call 911. I was trying to look around for Zaley, but Bert kept telling me not to move. It took the ambulance about twenty minutes to get there. The paramedics examined Zaley and suggested as a precaution they have her checked out at the emergency room. I remember being loaded into the ambulance. Bert told Shawn and his fiancée to go ahead with the wedding and then meet us at the emergency room. I was transported to a local hospital and then, a few hours later, transported to Jackson's hospital (JMCGH).

Dr. Chirqui, the neurosurgeon, examined me. She determined that I had very little feeling from the chest down. I had a little feeling in my right arm, but nothing else. I had no grip strength.

The diagnosis was that I had broken my neck at the C5 and C6 area. My spinal cord was not severed but severely bruised. These injuries resulted in paralysis from the chest down. I was classified as a quadriplegic. The only thing I could do was shrug my shoulders. My family was devastated by the news of my paralysis, but at least, I was alive. My daughter, Emily, has told me many times since my injury that she felt a tremendous blessing, because I had a broken body instead of a broken mind. She still had her mom, even though I could not move.

We were in the emergency room for a long time, as Dr. Chirqui continued to assess whether I needed emergency surgery at that time or if she could schedule the surgery for the next day. Several hours later, it was determined I would have surgery the next day. I was transferred to the neuro ICU.

The next morning, I had more tests run on me. After the tests, I would go to surgery. During one of the tests, they found a blood clot in my aortic arch. The doctors could not take the risk of the blood clot moving to my heart, so surgery was postponed until Wednesday.

My family was told that with this kind of injury, my body could continue to shut down.

Later that day I began to have trouble breathing. My blood pressure was also dropping.

Then sometime during the early morning hours, I came very near to dying. I do not know the medical definition of what happened. I just know it had something to do with too much medication; my body began to shut down. Things continued to spiral in the wrong direction. On Tuesday afternoon, I began having so much difficulty breathing that they had to do an emergency intubation. I could breathe again, but I could not talk.

The vent was the worst part of everything I was going through. I would wake up during the night, fighting to get it out of my mouth. Even today, if I see someone on television wearing a vent, I look away. All those memories wash over me like it was yesterday. I shudder now, as I write about it.

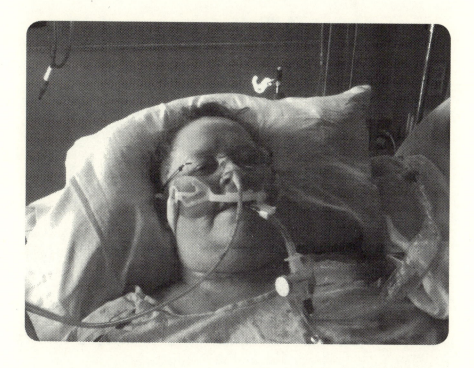

On Wednesday, I was finally stable enough to have the surgery on my neck. It took about seven hours and two surgeries. The team operated on the back of my neck first and then the front. Cadaver bone was used to fuse the vertebrae from C4 to T1. Rods were used on both sides. Ligaments were repaired in the front of my neck. Overall, the doctors felt the surgery went well.

As the days wore on, my family never knew what they were going to find when they would come for their morning visit. Each day it seemed there was something else happening with me. My blood pressure dropped, tube feedings had to be increased, the possibility of internal bleeding arose, etc. My breathing was labored, and they needed to do a tracheotomy, but they had to wait ten days to give my neck incision time to heal. On and on it went.

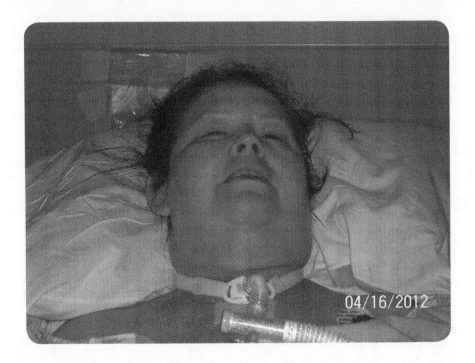

I had always thought that waiting through a patient's recovery was much harder for the family than for the patient, and now I believe it. The emotional stress must have been horrendous. I, on the other hand, was remarkably calm for someone who had broken her neck. The medication played a role in my calm demeanor, but there was something more. There was much, much more to this story.

I was in the Jackson hospital for almost a month. Family, friends, coworkers, and church members were so faithful with their visits. My family also bought red bracelets with Jeremiah 29:11 written on them. They wore these bracelets faithfully until I came home.

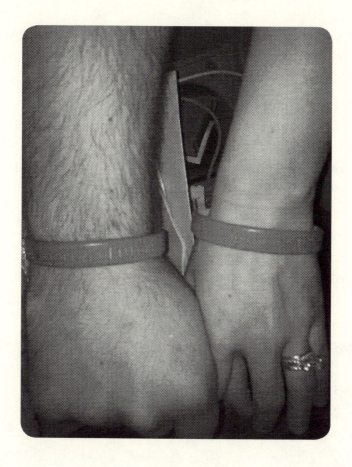

Seth and Hannah, my son and daughter-in-law, brought a radio and placed it in my room. Every night, at the end of the last visit, someone would turn the radio to K-LOVE, an awesome Christian radio station. The songs have encouraged me many times over the years. During the night, I would wake up, and I could hear the radio playing softly. The Christian band Mercy Me had released a song called "The Hurt and the Healer." This song seemed to speak to me. The lyrics described me so well. It became my song. Every night I would wake up and hear it playing. Emily told me that every time she drove to the hospital, she heard that song. I believe it was God's way of giving both of us strength to carry on.

It was so lonely after the last daily visitation. Bert was downstairs, where he spent every night, but it seemed that he was miles away. If he had been permitted, I know he would have been with me every minute. I could hardly wait for the next day's visitation time. I would watch the clock, counting the minutes. I have to say I was amazed at all the friends and coworkers who came to the hospital. Many of them were visibly upset when they came into the room and saw me. I wanted to comfort them, assure them everything was going to be okay, but I still had the vent, so I couldn't talk. Several people prayed over me during my stay in the hospital. They all meant so much to me. But the one that tugged at my heartstrings the most was the prayer spoken by my sixteen-year-old grandson, Vince. He is an amazing young man, and I am so proud of his walk with God.

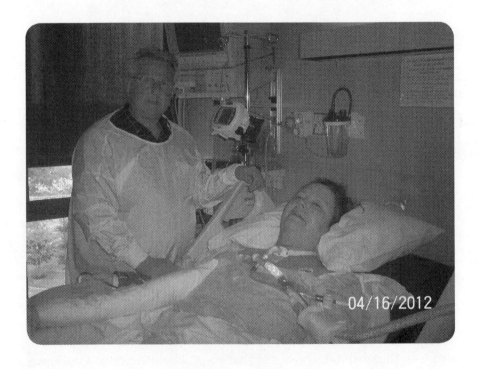

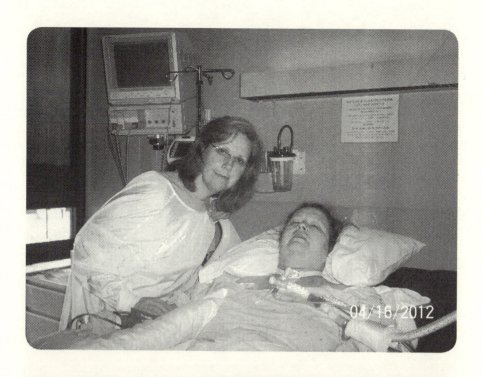

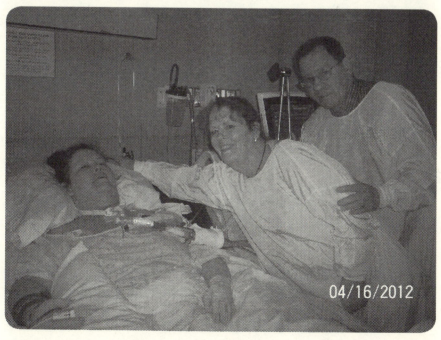

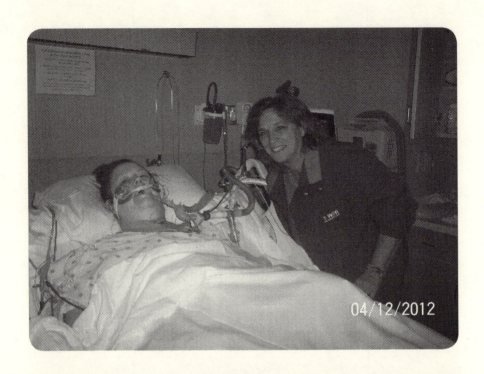

04/12/2012

04/18/2012

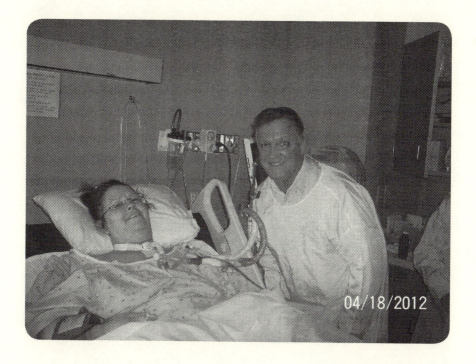

The hospital staff was wonderful to me. They brought a TV and DVD player to my room. They brought their DVDs for me to watch. A couple of the girls from the therapy department even painted my toenails. I felt like royalty. On my last day at Jackson, they brought me a gift. It was a small, colorful cross. I think of them every time I look at it. I will always appreciate and remember their kindness, especially my nurses, Amber, Jennie, and Gina. They went the extra mile for me even though their job didn't require it. My daughter-in-law, Hannah, is now a nurse at the same hospital. I believe she has the same compassion and caring as these nurses did. I expect one day someone will be writing about her in a book.

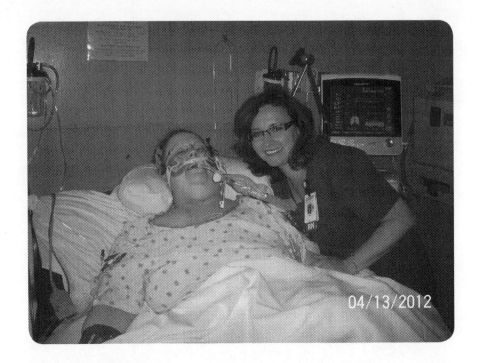

As the days turned into weeks, there was discussion as to where I would go for rehabilitation. I was still in ICU, but I was stable. It was important that I began my rehab as soon as possible. My family was told about spinal cord injury specialty hospitals. The two closest to us were Atlanta and Chicago. After researching both and praying over them, we felt God leading us to Atlanta. Our case manager, Kimberly, started the process of getting us accepted. It took her a couple of weeks to get everything set up, but we were finally ready to leave on April 24. Emily was taking a leave of absence from work, and she was flying down with me. Bert would be driving, so they would have transportation while they were there. They had projected I would be gone for eight weeks. We all knew it was something I had to do, but it was still a tearful good-bye. A new journey had begun, and I was trusting God to get my family and me through it.

After visiting hours on my last night at Jackson, I lay in the hospital bed and reflected on my life. I thought of all the ways God had been preparing us for the challenge ahead. My sister, who would later become a major caregiver for me, had moved from Missouri to Tennessee. She lived seven miles from my house. God knew I would need her. She had also taken an early retirement from her job the previous year. Bert was eligible to take early retirement, so he could be with me too. The house we lived in had all hardwood floors. The doorways were wide enough to get through, even though I did bang into a few door frames until I learned to maneuver my wheelchair.

There are so many more things I could name that made the transition easier. However, my point is that God will never send you without going before you to prepare the way. I am learning to trust God more every day. Is it easy? Not always. There are days I still wonder, *Why me?* I see others going about their normal days and remember when that was me.

Then I remember a time when I desperately asked God to help me, to take control of my life, and to make Him number one. Please let me say I do not believe God caused me to fall. I do believe He has used it for good. I became still before God and allowed Him to use me more sitting in this chair than I ever allowed Him to use me when I had been standing. Instead of saving me from drowning, He taught me to swim. He is number one in my life, and I give Him all the glory! He is taking me out of my comfort zone by prompting me to write this book. I am not an author, but God is going before me because I am convinced there is someone who needs to hear my story. So let me tell you a little more about me.

Chapter 2

Early Years

In the midfifties, my parents moved from Tennessee to Illinois to find work. It was fairly common during that time, and many Southerners hoped they could make a decent living in the booming city of Chicago. Most were farmers who wanted to get away from the long hours and low pay. Chicago gave them hopes and dreams of something better.

My parents had one child, my older brother, but had been trying to have a second child for several years. Mama was thirty-two, and Daddy was forty-one. As it typically goes, about the time they had given up on the idea, Mama found out she was expecting again. Nine months later, here I came. Since fathers were not allowed in the delivery room, the doctor normally came out to share the good news. In this case, the nurse came. Mama had delivered a healthy baby girl. But wait: there was more good news. Not only had she delivered a baby girl, but the doctor was also busy delivering another baby. Thirty-two minutes later, Mama gave birth to my identical twin, Darlene.

We moved back to Tennessee when we were about three years old. Daddy moved from job to job and moved us from house to house. There were many times Mama did not see her next house until Daddy moved us in. He made all the decisions, and Mama went along with it. She truly was a humble and kind woman.

Neither of my parents had much of an education. Mama quit school in the eighth grade and Daddy quit in the fourth. Daddy left home when he was ten years old. When we were young, we would sit for hours, listening to him tell stories about his younger years. He had a gift for storytelling, that's for sure.

My earliest childhood memory was when I was four years old. Funny thing about twins, that was Darlene's first memory too. It was Christmas. We each received a baby doll and a rocking chair. Mama said we spent many hours rocking our babies to sleep.

Those were happy days. We were too young to realize how poor we really were. The one thing we did know was that we had a wonderful, loving mother. Once we started to school, we began to notice that our lives were not quite the same as our classmates. Daddy's alcoholism had escalated. It didn't take much to figure out he was the reason we had so little. I always deeply resented him for that. Every year, the local Lions Club would bring a food basket to us at Thanksgiving, and if we were really lucky, they came back at Christmas with another basket. If you happen to be a member of the Lions Club, thank you. You have no idea what a difference you make! A few months ago, I was asked to speak at the local Lions Club. I took the opportunity to personally thank the organization for all the great things they do.

There were many times we received little or nothing at Christmas, but it was okay. I felt bad for Mama. I would see her crying, and I knew it was because she wasn't able to give us more. The houses we lived in were little more than shacks. You could actually see through the wood plank walls in a couple of the houses. That was not a big problem in the summer, since we didn't have air conditioning. The winter was a different story. The cold wind whipping through those cracks made for a pretty cold night. Most of the houses we lived in were heated by a coal stove, which was always placed in the living room. Darlene and I spent many hours bringing in coal to heat the house. The only time I ever heard my mama say a bad word was one day when Darlene and I were at the coal pile. I don't remember what started our fight, but when she bit me, I started chunking pieces of coal at her. She ran inside, and then Mama came to the door. Mama was normally a gentle soul, but that day she let loose on both of us. After that, I had a healthy fear of Mama.

One of my not-so-treasured memories was the memory of the outhouse. Until I left home, we only lived in one house that had indoor plumbing. Those cold winter mornings got a little bit colder after a quick trip to the outhouse! I do have to share one funny memory about the outhouse. When we were sixteen, Darlene decided she was going to start smoking. She chose the outhouse to be her hideaway from Mama and Daddy. Surprisingly, she didn't blow herself up from being around all the methane gasses. We did look out one day, and the outhouse looked like it was on fire. Smoke was billowing out of the roof vents. As you probably figured out, Mama found out her little secret.

Daddy's alcoholism continued to escalate, and in turn, his health worsened. He died when we were in our junior year of high school. He passed away at home in his sleep. He was fifty-eight. I didn't really know how I felt about Daddy dying. I had been angry at him for so many years because he had put his wants before his family's needs. In all honesty, I was a little relieved.

And I felt very, very guilty about it. The funeral was hard on Mama. Even though Daddy put her through so much during their marriage, she never stopped loving him. I can honestly say that she took her wedding vows seriously. She stood by him through it all. My mother was an amazing woman. She was a gentle, kind, and godly woman. Even though she had little by the world's standards, she felt rich in her heart. God had blessed her with children and grandchildren. That was enough for her. She passed away peacefully in her sleep at the age of eighty-one. Her plan was finished.

When I was fifteen, we lived beside Oakwood Baptist Church. I had never been to this church, but many from the neighborhood went there. The church had brought in a new pastor and family. The pastor's name was Tim. I always thought God brought that family just for me. Later I realized God brought them to do a work that would include me but was much, much bigger.

Tim was on fire for God, and very soon the church began to grow. My entire family joined the church, including my daddy. I do not know if Daddy gave his heart to Jesus, but I do remember him bowed down at the altar, crying like a baby. I pray that he became a child of God that day. Mama was a member of Oakwood until she passed away.

My brother was heavily involved in the bus ministry. Every Saturday they would visit neighborhoods, inviting families to church. If they didn't have transportation, the church bus would pick them up. The youth group was also growing. Tim started a youth choir, volleyball team, basketball team, and other activities. I was part of everything. For the first time in my life, I felt as good as everyone else. It didn't seem to matter to my youth group that I didn't have much. Tim had shown me that God loved me regardless of my circumstances. And I loved God with my whole heart.

Our church continued to grow under Tim's leadership. As I think back, I am not sure how Tim did so much. If all church members did a fraction of what some do, how many more souls would be living for Jesus? Tim's wife, Joyce, was also very involved in the church, plus raising two kids and a third on the way. God gave them strength beyond their wildest dreams. I will always be thankful for the constant spiritual support I received during the eleven years they were at our church. God used them to build my faith fundamentals. It was a major step in God's plan for my life. I speak with people all the time who feel they are not making a difference for God. Don't be disheartened. You may never know how much you have helped someone along the way, what a difference you've made. But that person knows. God doesn't make mistakes. Although Tim and Joyce picked up their family and all that was familiar to them and moved to a small church in rural West Tennessee, God was ahead of them preparing the way. Tim and Joyce, thank you for accepting God's call to be sent. We do serve an awesome God!

After I had graduated high school, I started college in the fall. All the scholarships I received at graduation were allowing me to attend nursing school at Union University. I was on top of the world. Then in late October, I became very sick and had to undergo surgery. Because of this, I would have to drop out of school for the semester, and I would also lose all my scholarship money. I knew then that I would have to get a job until the following fall semester. Hopefully, that would give me time to save enough money. I was fortunate enough to find a job quickly. I began my very first job working at Milan Hospital one month after the surgery.

While working at the hospital, I met someone, and after a whirlwind romance of six weeks, we married. He was seventeen, and I was eighteen. I started back to school in the fall as planned. It wasn't long until I realized I was pregnant. We both left school. He went to work, and I stayed home. A month after Emily was born, I also went to work. School was not an option at the time. Six years later, we had our son. I continued to work, putting school on the back burner.

I always hated that he wasn't able to graduate high school. Years later, the kids told me he received his GED. I was proud of him.

As in most marriages, we had our ups and downs. Marrying at such an early age did not help things. We both had a lot of growing up to do. Staying in church kept us on the right track. I believe marriages fail when focus is lost. I think of the apostle Peter when he got out of the boat to walk toward Jesus. As long as he kept his eyes on Jesus, he was fine. The minute he turned his eyes away, he began to sink. My favorite part of that story is the fact that Peter, at least, got out of the boat! So many times Jesus just wants us to step out of our comfort zones and trust Him with what's next.

I remember making a statement one day that had a serious effect on my life from that point on: "Satan might be able to do a lot of things, but he could never affect my marriage." He ripped it to shreds, and within a year, I was divorced. Please understand: God is much stronger than Satan. But you have to let God help you. He gives us choices. It is up to us to make the right choices. It seemed that one of us would try to make our marriage work, but the other wouldn't. Then the roles would reverse. Satan was continually in my ear, whispering to me, convincing me I deserved more from life. That is probably the biggest ploy Satan uses. By making us think we deserve bigger and better things, he makes us restless and dissatisfied. So we change our focus from God to ourselves.

As I look back at my life, all my happy moments were the moments I clung to God. No matter how low I sank, He was always there to pick me up. Do you ever wonder if God gets tired of helping us? I can tell you from experience He never tires of His children. He loves us unconditionally.

After my divorce, I was in and out of church. I was restless, looking for something but not wanting to admit I was really running from God. I would walk by my bookshelf and think my Bible was going to jump off the shelf and slap me on the head, which is exactly what I needed.

Running from God is an exhausting exercise. Why is it we always think we need to be in control? I had spent a big part of my life running away from the very thing I needed. It took more than ten years of running until I finally stopped.

In 2001, I married the love of my life. Besides my children, Bert is the best thing that has ever happened to me. With that marriage, I gained three wonderful sons and a granddaughter who has become more like a daughter to me. Blending two families is not always an easy task. I have to say ours blended better than most.

I started attending a wonderful church and immediately joined a Sunday school class. Connecting to a small group is so vital to staying in church. We need prayer warriors and a person to keep us accountable. I began teaching a women's Sunday school class a few years later. The class is my second family. Over the years we have laughed, cried, and prayed each other through many things. During the three months I was in the hospital, they continued to hold the class together. One of the first things I did, once I was able to speak again, was to call them during Sunday school. It was wonderful to hear their voices and all their words of encouragement. I wasn't sure if my health would allow me to keep teaching, but God has graciously allowed that to happen, and I am thankful for the continued opportunity to serve such wonderful women.

Chapter 3

Circumstances

Sometimes all we ever see is our own circumstances. I have heard the following statement made many times: Circumstances are ten percent what happens to you and ninety percent how you handle them. We can choose to trust God, or we can choose to be angry. If we choose anger, how do we move forward? If we choose trust, how do we move forward? Just because we trust God doesn't mean our circumstances have changed. Trusting God gives us hope that we don't have to do this alone. We exercise our faith muscles when we trust. I would probably be safe in saying that particular muscle is a little out of shape for most of us.

If we could pull back the curtain of life and see the big picture, then we might understand why God allowed us to be in this circumstance. Is that faith? We want life to be happy and without any trials. But how do we grow spiritually unless we go through those trials?

While in rehab at Shepherd Center, I was put through rigorous training every week. One of their objectives was to get you back into your life as much as possible. As part of that process, Jill (my physical therapist) wanted to train Emily to use the manual Hoyer lift to place me in the front seat of my car. We went to the parking garage for the training. Emily had to move the car to another parking spot to allow room for me and the lift. I am not sure what happened when I saw my car, but I began to feel overwhelmed. I became very quiet. The girls didn't notice at first, because they were busy getting me in the car. It seemed strange to me that I was sitting there in the front seat. It was as if the realization of everything I couldn't do had finally hit me.

Jill noticed how quiet I was and asked if I was okay. Emily slid into the driver's side of the car. She reached over and squeezed my hand. Jill whispered to me it was okay to cry, to mourn for everything I had lost. So I did. Sitting right there in my car with Emily and Jill beside me, I cried for the things I had lost, for the opportunities I would not have.

I still miss things about my old life, but my amazing family has worked hard to keep my life as normal as possible. My circumstances haven't changed. I am still in a wheelchair, but I am trusting God one day at a time.

Chapter 4

Shepherd Center

Shepherd Center in Atlanta, Georgia, was the hospital my family chose for my rehab. Chicago and Atlanta were both ranked in the top ten in the nation. This was so new to us that making the decision was difficult. I am sure Chicago had much to offer, but things were falling into place for us to go to Shepherd Center. This hospital was impressive from the moment we arrived. After the flight to Atlanta, they had an ambulance standing by to take me to Shepherd Center.

Since Emily and Bert were both taking a leave of absence from work, they were going to be with me during my stay at Shepherd. Bert was waiting at the hospital when we arrived. He wasn't the only one waiting. There was a room full of Shepherd employees ready to take care of me. I don't believe it ever slowed down from that point on. We were busy every day. But that was good. We didn't really have time to linger on the accident. They had you focused on getting better.

I was in ICU for the first nine days. They were finally able to remove the vent. That was a joyful day! I still had my trach, but they were reducing the size. My lungs were slowly healing from the pneumonia, and I was able to take deeper breaths. But my diaphragm didn't work well due to my paralysis, so I could not cough. Bert and Emily learned how to assist me as I learned how to cough. My lungs had to be suctioned out several times a day also.

I had not been able to speak for thirty days. Anyone who knows me knows this was probably more traumatic for me than not being able to move! The doctor decided my breathing was getting better, so the next step would be to put a talking tab on my trach. As they were putting the tab on, they told me it would take an hour or two before I could speak. I was very excited! We tend to take for granted little things, like talking, until we can no longer do it. My family had done a great job of reading my lips, and my mind in some cases. It was finally time. I had waited thirty days, so what was a couple more hours, right? Wrong! I was talking within twenty minutes.

Bert and Emily got to ICU about eight that morning, which was their normal time. When they came in, they greeted me as usual, expecting me to smile in response. And, boy, was I smiling. I watched their faces as I chirped right back with, "Good morning, how are you?" It was priceless. Emily started to cry. Bert turned away, but I had seen the tears. It was a moment we will all three remember. And of course, I haven't stopped talking since.

One thing that surprised us all was I sounded like me. With the trach in, we thought I might sound mechanical. I then started to call everybody I could think of. There were a lot of tears and laughter that day. We had taken a step forward in our journey. It did much to raise our spirits.

I believe everything happens for a reason. Seth had been scheduled to be in Atlanta for training six months earlier. For whatever reason, it kept getting rescheduled. The last rescheduled date was the first week of May, which was one week after I arrived at Shepherd Center. We were hoping I would be out of ICU by then, but I was waiting for a room to open up on the rehab floor. Visiting hours are normally more limited in a critical care area. Emily spoke with one of our nurses about Seth being here for just a week. They were wonderful about it. Since I was no longer considered critical, Seth was able to spend a few hours with me every night. I tried to be brave when he left, but I wasn't. I cried like a baby. I was still thankful that it worked out for him to be there for awhile. God and His timing are always perfect.

The next week I was able to move out of ICU to a regular room. I was ready for rehab. My first weekly schedule included physical, occupational, speech, and recreational therapy. It also included educational classes and a psychologist. I had very little free time except for weekends. I only had one or two hours of physical therapy on Saturday. On Sunday, the chapel was available for anyone interested. I smiled when I heard the pastor's name was Ben because my pastor's name was also Ben.

Shepherd also had a secret garden that patients and families could use when the weather was nice. We sat out there a few times, but it was a little too hot for Bert and Emily. It was only ninety-five degrees! What was the problem? After six weeks of being inside, I loved being outside again.

My rehab team was called the "Jill" team because five of the team members were named Jill. I had been told repeatedly the Jill team were superstars. I was anxious to get started but pretty nervous too. Everything that had happened since the accident had seemed surreal. I was no longer in control of anything. I was 100 percent dependent on everyone.

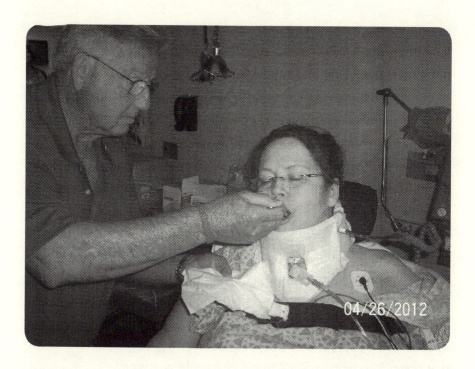

There was so much to learn. I was slowly beginning to move my hands and arms. Shepherd Center uses the sip-and-puff method to drive your wheelchair when you cannot use your hands. This was not my finest moment. I sipped when I should have puffed and vice versa. I just could not get it! Finally, the therapist set up a hand control for me to use. Until I could use my hands, they had to drive me back and forth to therapy. I slowly began to use my right hand, so I started to drive my wheelchair. Bert and Emily made sure they stayed out of my way for a while! The first time I used the hand controls, I ran over my hospital bed. Thankfully, I never ran over a person. At Shepherd, it was normal to see wheelchairs everywhere. It was as if we were cocooned from the real world.

One of the harder things for me to learn was how to back off the elevator. But Jill would make everyone on the elevator wait while I tried multiple times to back out. She was tough, and eventually I would get it. She was encouraging, but she didn't back down. I think we would have stayed on that elevator all day if that's what it had taken!

Each day I spent numerous hours in therapy. Besides therapy, I had daily educational classes. I also had to meet with a psychologist weekly. There were a few weeks I had to meet with the psychologist two times. Emily would laughingly tell me I wasn't passing the class, so they were making me repeat it. She also told me to get the answers right next class. My daughter has quite the sense of humor!

At Shepherd, they didn't give you much time to think about anything except getting better. Every day I was introduced to something new. The challenges continued to get harder. About the time I wanted to quit, I would accomplish the task. I still remember the first time I was able to push the page button on a Kindle. I felt as if I had won the lottery. There were many "firsts." Raising my arms, touching my chin, and scratching my nose were all victories. Every day seemed to bring with it hope for new beginnings.

Another requirement for all rehab patients was to participate in at least two outings per month. I didn't want to go anywhere, but no was not an option. Emily loves WNBA, and since Atlanta had a team, we decided that would be one of my outings. Although it was a little scary at first, we had a great time. For the other outing, I chose to go to the movie theater. Darlene and Kent had come to Atlanta to spend a few days, so she was going with us. I was pretty nervous about all of it, and I was glad she and Emily were both going. When we arrived the first test was to get through the door with my wheelchair. Once there, we headed into the theater. Darlene stopped for popcorn and drinks. There was a platform for us to use, with chairs on each side. We were running late, so the movie had already started. I kept trying to back up on the platform, but I couldn't see. By the time I finally got settled, I realized I was in the middle of the platform, far away from Darlene and Emily. Needless to say, I was a little frustrated. Once again, I realized my circumstances were different now. I could either accept the change or let it frustrate me.

It was another emotional good-bye when Darlene left at the end of the week. I wasn't ready to see her go, but I knew I should be home in less than a month. At this point, I had been away from home for two months. I was ready to go home!

Shepherd also required patients to participate in a weekly team activity. This involved every patient participating in a game, painting, or outside activity. On one particular day, I discovered we were all going to Chick-Fil-A. There were about fifteen of us. Each of us also could bring a family member. So here we went, single file in our wheelchairs down the streets of Atlanta. It felt good to be outside but a little scary too. The funny thing was that no one paid much attention to us. Shepherd Center had been doing this for so long, and everyone was accustomed to seeing lots of wheelchairs. Of course, Jill had thrown in a twist, which she was so good at. That was also the day she decided I would start driving my wheelchair with my left hand. I am left-handed, but my left side was much weaker than my right. I remember looking at her to see if she was kidding. When I saw her face, I knew she wasn't going to back down. At least, let me practice driving left-handed before we go. She gave me ten minutes! I surprised myself by making an eventless outing. I was able to get in and out of the restaurant without running over anyone. Jill and Emily were right there, encouraging me every step of the way.

The Jills were my biggest cheerleaders. They were also my pushers. I was able to do more than I ever expected. They celebrated my victories with me. I will always be grateful to them and others at Shepherd Center for helping me put my life back together.

I spent nine weeks at Shepherd. It became my safe haven. Being surrounded by people in wheelchairs was the norm. I was anxious to be home but a little concerned about making the transition. Bert had been working hard to get our home ready to accommodate me. So I knew everything was going to work out. It would just take time, and time was something I had plenty of.

Chapter 5

I'm Speaking! Are You Listening?

In the early part of my rehab when I couldn't speak, God reminded me of the lost art of listening. I am not sure if it is a lost art or a skill that we were never taught. In school, we were taught to read and write. Were we taught to listen?

Throughout my career as a human resources manager, I had many opportunities to listen. Employees were in and out of my office on a regular basis. Sometimes it was voluntary and sometimes not. I became a counselor of sorts. For many people, I was the one person who would be unbiased and listen to their problems without judging them. They needed me to listen. But I was not very good at it. On a scale of one to ten, I was maybe a two. Not a good score for someone in my field.

I began to pray that God would make me a better listener. Some might think this was not something to pray about. My belief is you should pray about everything. Every detail of your life is important to God. He wants to be in constant communication with us.

A few weeks after I began seeking God about my listening skills, He opened the door for me to start the process. My manager asked me to revise our current pay-for-skills program to include some team-building classes. My first thought was to include a listening-skills class. The best way to learn is to teach.

My research soon led me to the belief that listening was a very critical part of the communication process. In fact, we spend more time listening than any other form of communication. So learning how to listen was more important than ever.

If you conducted a survey, most people would say they were okay at listening. A few might even say they were pretty good at it. I decided to find out. I began to observe people around me. Some seemed to be very good listeners, while others didn't appear to hear anything spoken to them.

So what did it take to be a good listener? The first step was to *stop* talking! It is impossible to talk and listen at the same time. This, I soon concluded, was my biggest problem. I like to talk. My husband would agree! But during the thirty days I couldn't talk, he was the first to tell me how much he missed hearing me speak.

Have you ever had a one-sided conversation? The person you are speaking to is not engaged in the conversation. How can you tell? Maybe it's the deer-in-the-headlights look. Or maybe it's the blank stare. As a teacher/trainer, I have learned to recognize the signs. I know when they stop listening.

What makes them disengage? There are actually a number of reasons. Here are a few:

- no interest in the subject
- judging the person who is speaking
- planning what you want to say as soon as they stop talking
- disagreeing with the person speaking
- preoccupied with something else

Whatever the reason, listening skills can be improved with practice. Like most things, it takes effort to improve.

Every time I taught the listening-skills class, I felt I was learning as much as my students. Learning how to listen is a good thing, but putting it into practice is entirely different. For me, it took thirty days of silence. I began to pay more attention to conversations. I noticed the body language. But more than that, I began to listen deeper. I heard what they weren't saying. People are much more complex than they appear. We don't really know someone until we listen to them. We can pull back the layers and see the real person, the hurting person, the angry person, the person who needs Christ in his or her life. That was what God was trying to teach me.

Lying in a hospital room for weeks can be a great learning opportunity. God did his best work on me during that period of my life. Since I couldn't talk, I began to observe. I noticed that people talked more openly in front of me. Sometimes I even felt invisible to people. It was as if I couldn't hear since I couldn't speak. As I listened, I came to the conclusion there were a lot of unhappy people in the world.

When I began speaking again, I knew more than ever I wanted to glorify God with every word I spoke. I wanted to help others find real happiness. Happiness that only comes from God.

As Christians, we should be setting an example for others. The words we speak should build others up. Once we speak, we can't take it back. There have been countless times I wanted to take back something I said. Too late! The damage had been done. Feelings had been hurt.

God has taught me valuable lessons about speaking that I want to share with you. I pray you will receive the same blessings as I have received every time I practice them.

Before I speak, I use the acronym *TNK*. Is it *true*? Is it *necessary*? Is it *kind*? Please remember it has to fit all three criteria, not just one!

This one lesson has taught me so much. I have to admit I don't talk as much as I use to.

Another thing I have noticed about myself is how often I speak before my brain engages. If I had taken a moment to think about my response, I would most likely have said something different. Now, I try to apply the three-second rule. And you guessed it. It really works.

By following these two rules, God has shown me the power of words. Psalm 141:3 is a verse I memorized that has helped me many times. "Set a guard over my mouth, O Lord. Keep watch over the door of my lips."

Listening to others and speaking with compassion are examples Jesus gave us. He did this because He loves us from the inside out. When we love with a pure heart, we see others in a very different way, the way Jesus sees.

Chapter 6

He's Not Finished

Jeremiah 29:11

How do you put into words the emotions you feel when you encounter a moment that takes your breath away? My life changed forever by a freak accident. What was going to happen now?

It was late. The last visiting time had been over for awhile. The radio was playing my song by Mercy Me. "The Hurt and the Healer" had become a comfort to me. The nurses' station was right outside my room. I could see the nurses working quietly at their desks. I looked toward the door as a nurse stuck her head inside my door. She smiled and said hello. She went on to tell me everything was going to be all right. Then she was gone. What was she doing here? She wasn't one of my nurses. In fact, she wasn't a nurse at all. She looked exactly like Karen. She even had the long, curly hair like Karen's. Karen was my boss's wife. Was I seeing things? Was I dreaming? Whatever it had been it made me smile. I knew God sent her to me to give me reassurance that He had heard all the prayers on my behalf. And that was only the beginning of what God was up to.

As I was contemplating what I had just seen, a woman walked into my room. She sat down in a chair beside my bed. Where did that chair come from? It had not been there earlier. While I was trying to figure it out, something else caught my attention. I looked over to my right. I was no longer in my room. I was not really sure where I was. All I could see were dark clouds. As I watched the clouds, it reminded me of the many times I sat on my back porch and watched storm clouds. The clouds seemed to be moving fast. Suddenly there were white clouds looming above the dark clouds—beautiful, puffy, white clouds, clouds that reminded me of when I was a child and would try to identify the shapes.

I glanced back at the chair to my left to see if the woman was still there. She was sitting with her head bowed. I couldn't tell if she was reading or praying. She had a book opened in her lap. The book looked a little worn. The pages were dog-eared from excessive turning. It must have been her favorite. It reminded me a little of the Bible my mama used to have. I tried to see the woman's face, but it was very shadowy. From what I could make out, she was in her thirties. There was something about this woman that I couldn't quite put my finger on. She made me feel calm.

Still trying to figure everything out, I turned back to my clouds. There they were, still looming magnificently in the sky. As I continued to watch, I could see a light shining through the clouds. It was becoming brighter and brighter. It was breathtaking. I felt drawn to it. I didn't know what it was, but I knew it was good. It felt warm on my face. I wanted to close my eyes and bask in that warmth, but I couldn't take my eyes off of it.

Then I heard a voice. I swallowed hard as I blinked back the tears. This had to be a dream. *Was that really God's voice I heard?* I strained to look, but the light was too bright. As I tried to make sense of it all, I heard the voice again. And I knew—I was hearing the voice of God.

As I have shared this story with others, there has been one question that I have always been asked. What did God sound like? Gentle, kind, and warm were the adjectives that come to mind, but none really captured what I was hearing. Indescribable was the best way to describe it. Honestly, I was much more interested in *what* was being said.

God was speaking to me. He was asking me a question, and I was speechless. A question that had an easy answer. Are you ready to come home? The answer was yes! With every ounce of my being, I was ready. My broken body would be restored. I started to answer, but I stopped as I realized I was making this about me. Why was God giving me a choice? Was my time being cut short, or was it my time? As Christians, God gives us his Holy Spirit to guide us. It whispers to us, nudges us in the right direction.

My very favorite verse in the Bible is Jeremiah 29:11, which says, "For I know the plans I have for you, saith the Lord. Plans to prosper you and not to harm you. Plans for a future and a hope" (NIV). As I thought about my answer, this verse came to my mind. Had I completed God's plan? I wanted to. God had given His son for me. I owed him so much.

I felt I had to know. *Was there more I could do?* I heard God gently whisper His reply. There was more for me to do. The choice was mine. Immediately I knew my choice was made. I would stay and finish what God had planned for me.

As I made my choice I watched the woman seated in the chair. She stood up and smiled at me as she turned to leave. Instantly I knew who she was and why she was there! It was my mama, and she had come to take me home if I had chosen to do so. What a sweet moment. I wanted to call her back just for a little while. But I knew one day I would see her again, and we could spend eternity together.

I do believe that when she smiled at me, she was letting me know she was proud of me for the decision I had made to stay.

There are many things I don't understand about that night. More than anything else, I wonder why I was given a choice, a second chance to complete the perfect plan God has for me. One day as I humbly bow before Him, I will understand. But for now, I made a promise I intend to keep—a promise to finish the plan.

I am amazed daily at how God goes before us in our journey. When I first felt God leading me to write a book, I thought, *I know nothing about writing a book*. Our inability has never stopped God. I put it off for over a year, until one day I knew I would not have peace until I wrote this book. I began to pray that God would give me the words. I wanted to glorify Him with my words.

The people who God places in our path are not there by coincidence. They are there for a reason. Some are more memorable than others. You might even make a lasting impression on someone. Hopefully, that is a good thing. I am afraid I have left a few not-so-good impressions in my lifetime.

My husband and I were working with a realtor recently. As we began to talk, we found that his daughter was also in a wheelchair. I told him about the book I was writing and showed him the book's cover. It was as if it stirred a memory for him, and he began to tell me about his daughter's accident.

She was in a car accident several years ago. After more than four months in a coma, she woke up. It took awhile for her to be able to speak. When she did, she had a profound story to tell. She was scared when she first had the accident, until she went to heaven. There were three angels. She described each one in detail. They sang songs to her, which calmed her down. As they were singing, she saw her grandfather, and she wasn't scared anymore. The light was so bright, and then suddenly she saw Jesus. He was standing before her. He asked if she was ready to come home. She told her parents she really, really wanted to say yes.

But then she thought about her mom. She knew her dad would be okay, but her mom would struggle without her. She told Jesus she wasn't ready to come home. He then told her that if she stayed, she would have to live for Him.

As I relayed this story to my daughter, she blinked back tears. She admitted that before my injury, she had been skeptical whenever she heard of someone having an encounter with God. Now, to hear an almost identical story to mine washed away any doubts she had ever had. For me, hearing this girl's story brought back my own story vividly.

Does everyone get a choice to return? I don't know. I know I did. I believe when you have finished the plan, God will take you home. My mama was an example of someone who, I believe, finished God's plan for her life. She loved children. Each grandchild and great-grandchildren had his or her own special time with Mama. Two weeks after the youngest great-grandchild started school, Mama passed away. She died peacefully in her sleep. When we saw her, she had the most angelic look on her face. I believe she was looking in the face of Jesus!

I know there will always be skeptics who don't quite believe. All I can say is Heaven is for real. God has prepared a place for all who accept Him. Please don't delay your relationship with God. The good life is waiting for us on the other side.

Chapter 7

Home Sweet Home

June 21, 2012, it was finally here. After almost three months in hospitals, I was finally going home. Emily had been marking off the days on a big calendar. Everyone kept asking, with a laugh, if we were that tired of them. We were quick to assure them we would miss them very much. They were such a big part of our lives now. If I could have taken them home with me, I would have gladly done so.

I had slept very little the previous night in anticipation of our trip home. I had not been there since April 1. It seemed like forever. Today I was returning in my wheelchair. It was going to be a bittersweet day. My family would be gathering there to greet me. I knew there were going to be many adjustments ahead for all of us.

Bert went home for a week at the end of May so he could line up all the work that had to be done to make our house handicap accessible. He also had to sell our SUV and find a handicap-accessible van. We laughingly told our children that we were spending their inheritance.

I missed Bert terribly the week he was gone. We had become accustomed to being together during most of my waking hours. The good part was that Darlene and Kent came up the week he was gone.

It had been very difficult not being able to see my sister when I wanted to. We only lived seven miles from each other. So I was really looking forward to their visit. I told myself I wouldn't cry when she left, but I did. I wanted to go home, but I still had another month in rehab. I will always remember what Bert said when he returned to Shepherd Center. I asked him if it was great being home. He looked at me and said, "I am home now. Wherever you are is home to me." How sweet is that!

I am very glad my husband is a detail person. There was so much involved in getting everything ready for me. When he came back to the hospital the next week, I was overwhelmed by everything he was telling me he had achieved during such a short time. He had left Shawn and Darlene to oversee the work inside the house.

There were two men, Mike and Frank, who had offered to build a ramp for me. They had worked for Bert a few years ago, and now they had their own construction company. They installed the ramp during the week Bert was home. After they had finished the ramp, they refused payment. What a nice surprise. At least, we knew I could get in the house when I returned home.

Bert was able to buy a handicap-accessible van while he was home, but it had to be fitted with the lift so he could not drive it back. Someone was going to drive the van to Atlanta when it was ready. That surprised me because Atlanta was a six-hour trip. Every few days Bert would call them to check the progress of the lift. Finally, we were down to our final week, and the van was still not ready. Bert was not happy. It was Monday, and we were leaving on Friday. When he tried to contact the salesman, he was told the salesman was on vacation. No one seemed to know what was going on with the van. We were going home in four days, but I had no way to get there. We still had our SUV, but we didn't have room for my wheelchair. After numerous phone calls, another salesman rented us a van. They were driving it to Atlanta and taking our SUV back with them. Although

Bert was frustrated that our new van was not ready, at least, we had a way home.

Shepherd Center always holds a graduation ceremony for each patient before he or she leaves. On Wednesday, it was my turn. The patient gets to pick a theme song. As it is played, everyone in the rehab gym gathers around to help you celebrate your special day. I chose for my theme song a Mandisa song titled "Good Morning." This was so appropriate for me because she sang about starting a brand-new day, and that was exactly what I was doing.

After the graduation ceremony, I had rehab for the last time at Shepherd Center. As I anticipated, Jill did not take it easy on me!

The next morning, we said our good-byes, then Bert and Emily packed up the van, and we were ready to go by 8:00 a.m. Bert was not at all happy with the van they had delivered the day before. He was just hoping it would get us back to Tennessee.

The first part of the trip went pretty well. We had to stop every two hours so I could do a weight shift to keep from getting pressure sores. Normally, this needs to be done every thirty minutes, but for short-term purposes, we could extend it.

As we were coming into Nashville, Bert noticed the van began to sound sluggish. By the time we left Nashville, the van could barely get up the steep hills. We decided to stop at the next exit. But before we could get there, the van just stopped. Bert was barely able to get it to the shoulder of the road. We were four miles from the next exit, and it was ninety-five degrees outside.

One of the things we had been taught about my condition was that my body cannot regulate temperatures. I needed to avoid excessive heat or cold. I could tell Bert and Emily were both concerned. Emily opened the van door and dropped the ramp open. We both just stared. The ditch was at least four feet deep. It was a little unnerving to know I could not get out of the van.

After waiting over two hours, we finally got a wrecker from Nashville to pick us up. Bert told the driver I could not get out of the van, so he loaded us up on his flatbed wrecker. It was certainly a new experience for all of us. I had never ridden in a wrecker, much less been loaded on it! The next exit was only four miles away. There was a Goodyear store located there. My daughter knew the owner, and he had promised to look at the van pretty quick.

As we took our exit we could see a homeless man at the stop sign. He had a sign asking for help. We were sitting up so high we could not have helped him even if we had planned to. I am sure we looked a little like the Beverly Hillbillies, except my rocking chair was a wheelchair. He continued to stare at us as we approached the stop. I could tell he was contemplating saying something. Finally, he started to yell, "That's against the law! You need to get down because that's against the law," Emily just smiled at him until we passed him. Then we all burst out laughing. Some of the tension of the day drained away.

Pretty soon, we learned the van could not be repaired for a few days. Now we had to wait for another van. It was closing time at the Goodyear store, but they were gracious enough to keep the store open until our van arrived. We arrived home, tired but happy, at 8:30 p.m. It had been a very long day. Our family was patiently waiting, and we were so excited to see everyone.

Chapter 8

Where Do We Go from Here?

Being in a wheelchair has been a challenge in so many ways. Without God walking with me every step of the way, I would not feel the hope that I do. I know God is using me, and it feels good. All the troubles we go through can be turned into something good. Some of the most touching testimonies I have heard came from people who overcame some kind of obstacle.

Ten days after I arrived home, I was able to attend church again. I also taught Sunday school for the first time in four months. It was such a sweet homecoming. I did have a few problems in the beginning. I could not talk for long periods without losing my breath. My lung capacity is much better now. I can almost sneeze like a normal person. I still have trouble coughing, but it is better.

Before I had my accident, I rarely went to the doctor. Now I seem to go all the time. Therapist and nurses are in my home weekly. I know that every person I cross paths with is there for a reason. I have listened, prayed, and even counseled a few along the way in the last eighteen months. I know my life is a little better for having met them.

There is little to no chance I will ever walk again. Guess I'll have to wait until I walk with Jesus. I have developed more use of my arms and hands. My fingers don't have much movement. I can use my thumb and index finger on my left hand. In fact, I typed this book with one finger. Yes, it was mighty slow at times.

Getting back the use of my muscles is somewhat comparable to the growth of children. I have two grandchildren I am competing with. Kinley is two, and Zaley is almost two. As I have watched them grow over the last eighteen months, I realized we were learning very similar things. They are about to surpass me, but I still try to keep up. Those two little girls will never remember me before my wheelchair. But that's okay; I can enjoy watching them grow and fill my lap with toys! From time to time, Kinley will ask me to go upstairs with her. I explain I cannot because my legs don't work. She immediately grabs her legs and proclaims that her legs don't work either! It always makes me smile.

In the last few weeks during Sunday school, I have been teaching a series called "Sent." It is about churches going out to spread God's word. Unfortunately today, most church members want you to come to them and get a little picky about who they want. The early church had the right idea. Go and spread the word. That doesn't mean you have to go to another country. It could be across the street. The idea is to go where God sends you. If each of us would wake up every day and say to God, "Here am I—send me," think of all the lives we could touch

So what has this got to do with where I am going? Everything! I am making a conscious decision to pray, "Here am I—send me, wheelchair and all."

God gave me a second chance eighteen months ago. I want to live each day in the center of God's plan for me. I pray that you will seek Him and His plan for your life. Then get ready for the most satisfying time of your life!

God bless.